The Meaning of Christmas

By
Mary Kaye

BLACK FOREST PRESS
San Diego, California
December, 2000
First Edition

The Meaning of Christmas

By
Mary Kaye

PUBLISHED IN THE UNITED STATES OF AMERICA
BY
BLACK FOREST PRESS
P.O. Box 6342
Chula Vista, CA 91909-6342
1-800-451-9404

**Illustrations By
Karl T. Yu**

**Graphic Design By
G. Robert O'Barts Jr.**

No part of this publication may be reproduced in whole or part, or stored in a retrieval system, or transmitted in any form or by any means, electronic, mechanical, photocopying, recording, or otherwise, without written permission of the author/publisher. For information regarding permission, write to Mary Kaye, Streets of Gold Enterprises, P.O. Box 22023, Phoenix, AZ 85028.

Text copyright © 1989, 1999
Illustrations copyright © 1998 by Karl T. Yu
All rights reserved.
Streets of Gold Enterprises

Printed in U.S.A.

(All scripture notations are King James Version.)

Disclaimer

This document is an original work of the author. It may include reference to information commonly known or freely available to the general public. Any resemblance to other published information is purely coincidental. The author has in no way attempted to use material not of her own origination. Black Forest Press disclaims any association with or responsibility for the ideas, opinions or facts as expressed by the author of this book.

Printed in the United States of America
Library of Congress
Cataloging-in-Publication

ISBN: 1-58275-023-8
Copyright © December, 2000 by Mary Kaye
ALL RIGHTS RESERVED

"For God so loved the world, that he gave his only begotten Son, that whosoever believeth in him (Jesus) should not perish, but have everlasting life."

John 3:16

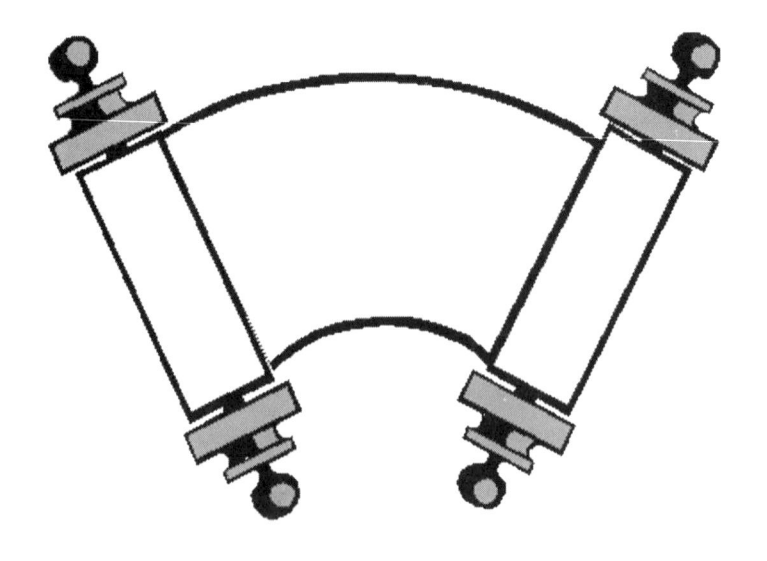

"As he spake by the mouth of his holy prophets, which have been since the world began: that we should be saved from our enemies…" -*Luke 1:70-71*

"…I the Lord am thy Saviour and thy Redeemer..."
-*Isaiah 49:26*

'Twas the meaning of Christmas
In that all through the land,
"A Savior!"
Prophets foretold by God's hand.

The Scriptures were passed
Down the ages it's clear,
In faith, the Redeemer
Soon would appear.

"...because there was no room for them in the inn."   -*Luke 2:7*

The people were already
Tucked into beds,
But Joseph and Mary
Found no place for their heads.

Then an innkeeper let them
Stay in a barn,
With hay and their blankets
To help them keep warm.

"...for we have seen his star in the east..."   *-Matthew 2:2*

"Behold, a virgin shall be with child, and shall bring forth a son...and thou shalt call his name JESUS: for he shall save his people from their sins."   *-Matthew 1:23/21*

When high up above
There arose such a star,
That people gazed up
From both near and afar.

Away in a stable,
The virgin gave birth
To the Promised Christ Child;
God here on earth!

"Now when Jesus was born in Bethlehem of Judaea in the days of Herod the king, behold, there came wise men from the east to Jerusalem, Saying, where is he that is born King of the Jews? for we have seen his star in the east, and are come to worship him."
"When Herod the king had heard these things, he was troubled..."   *-Matthew 2:1-3*

"And there were in the same country shepherds abiding in the field, keeping watch over their flock by night. And, lo, the angel of the Lord came upon them, and the glory of the Lord shone round about them: and they were sore afraid. And the angel said unto them, Fear not..."   *-Luke 2:8-10*

The Savior was born
In Bethlehem town,
And the talk of *this* King
Made King Herod frown...

When what, to the shepherds eyes,
Did appear,
But an angel of the Lord, who said,
"Have no fear...

"...behold, I bring you good tidings of great joy, which shall be to all people." *Luke 2:10*

"And this shall be a sign unto you; Ye shall find the babe wrapped in swaddling clothes, lying in a manger." *Luke 2:12*

"And they came with haste, and found Mary, and Joseph, and the babe lying in a manger. And when they had seen it, they made known abroad the saying which was told them concerning this child." *Luke 2:16-17*

"...he that is born King of the Jews..." *Matthew 2:2*

Behold, I bring you
Good tidings of great joy."
And they found Christ the Lord
A swaddled Baby Boy.

More rapid than eagles,
They spread the good news--
Born this day, a Savior,
The King of the Jews!

Hallelujah!

"And suddenly there was with the angel a multitude of the heavenly host praising God, and saying, Glory to God in the highest and on earth peace, good will toward men."
-Luke 2:13-14

"...This day is this scripture fulfilled in your ears."
(-Jesus) -Luke 4:21

"And all they that heard it wondered at those things which were told them by the shepherds." *-Luke 2:18*

"...behold there came wise men from the east to Jerusalem, Saying, Where is he that is born King of the Jews? for we have seen his star in the east, and are come to worship him." *-Matthew 2:1-2*

"...they presented unto him gifts; gold, and frankincense, and myrrh." *Matthew 2:11*

Praise God! Give glory!
Peace and good will!
Worship Him! Bless Him!
The Prophecy fulfilled!

And all that heard wondered
At those things that were told.
And the wise men brought gifts
Of resins and gold.

"...the angel of the Lord appeareth to Joseph in a dream, saying, Arise, and take the young child and his mother and flee into Egypt, and be thou there until I bring thee word for Herod will seek the young child to destroy him. When he arose, he took the young child and his mother by night, and departed into Egypt." -*Matthew 2:13-14*

"...and they shall call His name Emmanuel, which being interpreted is, God with us." -*Matthew 1:23*

Then the angel of the Lord
Appeared to Joseph in a dream,
And foretold of Herod's
Murderous scheme.

So down into Egypt,
By night, the three flew:
Joseph and Mary
And Emmanuel, too.

"Then Herod, when he saw that he was mocked of the wise men, was exceeding wroth, and sent forth, and slew all the children that were in Bethlehem and in all the coasts thereof, from two years old and under..."   *Matthew 2:16*

And then, the mocked king
Was exceedingly mad.
(He knew, that by wise men,
He had been had.)

So he sent forth and slew
All the children asunder,
In Bethlehem, her coasts,
Ages two years and under.

"But when Herod was dead, behold, an angel of the Lord appeareth in a dream to Joseph in Egypt, saying, Arise, and take the young child and his mother, and go into the land of Israel for they are dead which sought the young child's life. And he arose, and took the young child and his mother, and came into the land of Israel. But when he heard that Archelaus did reign in Judaea in the room of his father Herod, he was afraid to go thither notwithstanding, being warned of God in a dream, he turned aside into the parts of Galilee." *Matthew 2:19-22*

Then Joseph saw the angel
When Herod was dead:
"Arise, take the child
And his mother," he said,

"And into the land of Israel,
Go forth..."
And God, in a dream,
Showed the way north.

"And he came and dwelt in a city called Nazareth: that it might be fulfilled which was spoken by the prophets, He shall be called a Nazarene." -Matthew 2:23

"And the child grew, and waxed strong in spirit, filled with wisdom: and the grace of God was upon him." -Luke 2:40

So the family went to Nazareth
Of Galilee,
Fulfilling, yet another,
Prophecy:

That Jesus shall be called
A Nazarene.
He grew in spirit,
In wisdom, and grace supreme.

"And Jesus himself began to be about thirty years of age..."
-Luke 3:23

"And great multitudes came unto him, having with them those that were lame, blind, dumb, maimed, and many others, and cast them down at Jesus' feet; and he healed them." *Matthew 15:30*

"...behold, there was a dead man carried out, the only son of his mother, and she was a widow: and many people of the city was with her...And he (Jesus) said, Young man, I say unto thee, Arise. And he that was dead sat up, and began to speak. And he delivered him to his mother."
-Luke 7:12/14-15

"For he (Jairus) had one only daughter, about twelve years of age, and she lay a-dying. But as he (Jesus) went the people thronged him...While he yet spake, there cometh one from the ruler of the synagogue's house, saying to him, (Jairus) Thy daughter is dead; trouble not the Master. ...and (Jesus) took her by the hand, and called, saying, Maid, arise. And her spirit came again, and she arose straightway..." *-Luke 8:42/49/54-55*

"...(for his name was spread abroad)..." *-Mark 6:14*

Now when Jesus
Was about 30 years old,
He healed multitudes,
It is told:

Diseases. Plagues.
The blind. The lame.
He even raised the dead,
And so spread His name.

"Then drew near unto him all the publicans and sinners for to hear him. And the Pharisees and scribes murmured, saying, This man receiveth sinners, and eateth with them."
-Luke 15:1-2

"...and in him is no sin." *-I John 3:5*

"for with the heart man believeth unto righteousness..."
-Romans 10:10

"That Christ may dwell in your hearts by faith..."
-Ephesians 3:17

"If I then, your Lord and Master, have washed your feet; ye also ought to wash one another's feet. For I have given you an example, that ye should do as I have done to you."
-John 13:14-15

"...they were all with one accord..." *-Acts 2:1*

He dined with sinners,
Yet in Him is no sin.
(For it is our hearts,
He desires to win.)

He washed His disciples' feet
'Tho He was their Lord,
As an example to be like Him,
And all of one accord.

"...I (Jesus) seek not mine own will, but the will of the Father which hath sent me."   *-John 5:30*

"Heaven and earth shall pass away: but my words shall not pass away."   *-Luke 21:33*

"...except ye repent, ye shall all likewise perish."
-Luke 13:3/5

"...but these things I (Jesus) say, that ye might be saved."
-John 5:34

"In the beginning was the Word, and Word was with God, and the Word was God." "And the Word was made flesh, and dwelt among us..." " He was in the world, and the world was made by him, and the world knew him not."
-John 1:1/14/10

"Jesus answered and said unto him, Verily, verily, I say unto thee, Except a man be born again, he cannot see the kingdom of God."   *-John 3:3*

He spoke many words,
As He did His Father's will;
Of repentance, salvation--
The words live on still.

He was God in the flesh,
Down here on earth,
To give all who accept Him
A spiritual rebirth.

"Then Pilate therefore took Jesus, and scourged (whipped) him. And the soldiers platted a crown of thorns, and put it on his head…" -*John 19:1-2*

"And the men that held Jesus mocked him, and smote him. And when they had blindfolded him, they struck him on the face, and asked him, saying, Prophesy, who is it that smote thee?" -*Luke 22:63-64*

"And they spit upon him" -*Matthew 27:30*

"And he bearing his cross went forth..." -*John 19:17*

"And they crucified him…" *Matthew 27:35*

"Then said Jesus, Father, forgive them; for they know not what they do..." -*Luke 23:34*

"He is not here, but is risen. Remember how he spake unto you when he was yet in Galilee, Saying, The Son of man must be delivered unto the hands of sinful men, and be crucified, and the third day shall rise again." -*Luke 24:6-7*

"...this is indeed the Christ, the Saviour of the world." -*John 4:42*

But we whipped Him, beat Him,
Mocked Him and such.
He spread out His arms:
'I love you this much.'

Then He died on a cross,
BUT AROSE THREE DAYS LATER!
Merry Christmas to all.
MAY CHRIST BE YOUR SAVIOR!

"Behold, I (Jesus) stand at the door, and knock: if any man hear my voice, and open the door, I will come in to him, and will sup with him, and he with me."   -*Revelation 3:20*

WHAT MUST I DO TO BE SAVED?

1. Tell God that you have sinned.

2. Be willing to turn from sin.
   (Ask God to help you.)

3. Believe that Jesus died for you (as a sacrifice for all sins) and rose from the dead.

4. Ask God to save you. Believe He saved you and thank Him.

5. Ask Jesus to be the Lord of every area of your life.

Scripture for "What Must I Do To Be Saved"

"…what must I do to be saved? …Believe on the Lord Jesus Christ, and thou shalt be saved…" **Acts 16:30-31**

"There is none righteous, no, not one:" **Romans 3:10**

"For all have sinned, and come short of the glory of God;" **Romans 3:23**

"But God commendeth his love toward us, in that, while we were yet sinners, Christ died for us." **Romans 5:8**

"But now (God) commandeth all men every where to repent:" **Acts 17:30**

"If we confess our sins, he is faithful and just to forgive us our sins, and to cleanse us from all unrighteousness." **I John 1:9**

"And ye know that he was manifested to take away our sins…" **I John 3:5**

"Knowing that Christ being raised from the dead dieth no more; death hath no more dominion over him." **Romans 6:9**

"That if thou shalt confess with thy mouth the Lord Jesus, and shalt believe in thine heart that God hath raised him from the dead, thou shalt be saved. For with the heart man believeth unto righteousness, and with the mouth confession is made unto salvation." **Romans 10:9-10**

"But as many as received him, to them gave he power to become the sons of God, even to them that believe on his name: which were born, not of blood, nor of the will of the flesh, nor of the will of man, but of God." **John 1:12-13**

"And because ye are sons, God hath sent forth the Spirit of his Son into your hearts." **Galatians 4:6**

"…God hath given to us eternal life, and this life is in his Son." **1 John 5:11**

"Likewise, I (Jesus) say unto you, there is joy in the presence of the angels over one sinner that repenteth." **Luke 15:10**

Scripture Verses For Children

COMMANDMENTS:

"Children, obey your parents in the Lord: for this is right."
Ephesians 6:1

"Honor thy father and mother." *Ephesians 6:2*

"My son, keep thy father's commandment, and forsake not the law of thy mother." *Proverbs 6:20*

"And whatsoever ye do, do it heartily, as to the Lord, and not unto men." *Colossians 3:23*

"Jesus said…Thou shalt love the lord thy God with all thy heart, and with all thy soul, and with all thy mind. This is the first and great commandment. And the second is like unto it, Thou shalt love thy neighbor as thyself." *Matthew 22:37-39*

"Be swift to hear, slow to speak, slow to wrath." *James 1:19*

"Do all things without murmurings and disputings."
Philippians 2:14

"Let no corrupt communication proceed out of your mouth"
Ephesians 4:9

"Be ye angry and sin not; let not the sun go down upon your wrath." *Ephesians 4:6*

"Thou shalt not bear false witness against thy neighbour."
Exodus 20:16

"In every thing give thanks: for this is the will of God in Christ Jesus concerning you." *I Thessalonians 5:18*

"And be ye kind one to another, tenderhearted, forgiving one another, even as God for Christ's sake hath forgiven you."
Ephesians 4:32

PROMISES:

"For it is God which worketh in you both to will and to do of his good pleasure." ***Philippians 2:13***

"As for these four children, God gave them knowledge and skill in all learning and wisdom." ***Daniel 1:17***

"He which hath begun a good work in you will perform it until the day of Jesus Christ." ***Philippians 1:6***

"I can do all things through Christ which strengtheneth me." ***Philippians 4:13***

"For by grace are ye saved through faith; and that not of yourselves: it is the gift of God." ***Ephesians 2:8***

"Christ…is our life." ***Colossians 3:4***

"For in him we live, and move, and have our being."
Acts 17:28

"Therefore if any man be in Christ, he is a new creature: old things are passed away; behold, all things are become new." ***II Corinthians 5:17***

"For we are his workmanship, created in Christ Jesus unto good works." ***Ephesians 2:10***

"As the Father hath loved me, so have I (Jesus) loved you: continue ye in my love." ***John 15:9***

"For the Father himself loveth you…" ***John 16:27***

"I will both lay me down in peace and sleep: for thou,LORD, only makest me dwell in safety" ***Psalm 4:8***

"Jesus saith unto him, I am the way, the truth, and the life."
John 14:6

"All things work together for good to them that love God." ***Romans 8:28***

WORDS OF WISDOM:

"Even a child is known by his doings, whether his work be pure, and whether it be right." ***Proverbs 20:11***

"I delight to do thy will, O my God: yea, thy law is within my heart." ***Psalm 40:8***

"For by him (Jesus) were all things created, that are in heaven, and that are in earth… all things were created by him and for him.." ***Colossians 1:16***

"Know ye that the LORD he is God; it is he that hath made us." ***Psalm 100:3***

A soft answer turneth away wrath: but grievous words stir up anger." ***Proverbs 15:1***

"The LORD hate(s)…a proud look, a lying tongue…A false witness that speaketh lies" ***Proverbs 6:16/17/1*9**

"Whosoever hateth his brother is a murderer." ***I John 3:15***

"But the fruit of the Spirit is love, joy, peace, long-suffering, gentleness, goodness, faith, Meekness, temperance: against such there is no law." ***Galatians 5:22-23***

"That I may know him, and the power of his resurrection." ***Philippians 3:10***

"Finally, brethren, whatsoever things are true…honest…just…pure…lovely…are of good report; if there be any virtue…any praise, think on these things." ***Philippians 4:8***

"And there are also many other things which Jesus did, the which, if they should be written every one, I suppose that even the world itself could not contain the books that should be written. Amen." *-John 21:25*

Bible Quiz

1. Why did Joseph and Mary go to Bethlehem?

2. Why was Baby Jesus placed in a manger?

3. Who named Jesus? What does His name mean?

4. What does "Emmanuel" mean?

5. Who told the shepherds about the Savior, the Christ?

6. What led the Wise Men to Jesus?

7. Why was King Herod mad?

8. Where did Jesus grow up?

9. How old was Jesus when he began to heal people?

10. Why did Jesus die?

11. What happened after three days?

12. Where is Jesus now?

Our Christmas Traditions

Our Christmas Traditions

Christmas Memories

Christmas Memories

Favorite Scriptures

Favorite Scriptures

Favorite Scriptures

Favorite Scriptures

People in our Family

People in our Family

Prayer Requests

Answered Prayer

Prayer Requests

Answered Prayer

Special Notes

Special Notes